My Faith, My Poetry

– In Two Sets –

A Day In The Life

Come Running

Gary A. Burlingame

Healthy Life Press
Arvada, Colorado

My Faith, My Poetry

Photos and Cover Design
by Gary A. Burlingame

Library of Congress Cataloging-in-Publication Data

Burlingame, Gary A. (1958 -)
My Faith, My Poetry

ISBN 978-1939267221

1. Poetry
2. Inspirational & Religious Poetry

Second edition, 2017

Printed in the United States of America

Published by Healthy Life Press. Most Healthy Life Press resources are available worldwide through bookstores and online outlets, depending on their format. This book also exists in a downloadable and printable PDF from www.healthylifepress.com. Multiple copy discounts may be arranged by contacting the publisher at the address above, or by e-mailing: INFO@HEALTHYLIFEPRESS.COM.

Dedication

I dedicate this book of poems to my dad and my mom, John and Betty Burlingame, who raised me in a loving home, giving me constant support and encouragement to achieve whatever I set my mind and heart to do.

Revelation 22:1-5

Contents

Dinner Together
We Need Family
Dear Jesus
Not to be Distinguished
I Need You in My Life
Crown of Glory

Evening Chaos
Marriage is Hard Work
Wrestling for Control
Things on My List
Think Like I Think
You are the One
Trust Me
If Ever There was a Night

Bedtime
At the End of the Day
Look Beyond Me
That's What Daddies Do
God's Gift to a Lonely World
Like Solomon's Pomade
Eternal Love Divine

Set 2 – Come Running 63

All About Change
In His Image
Earth and Body
Get On With It
Extinction
Fix Your Thoughts on Me
Cup Bearer

Until You Came to Me
Wake Up, Rise Up
Cause Me to Grow
Maturity
Mystery of Mysteries
'Isms
Who Pursues Whom?
Better to Receive
Why Did You Go?
Clay Reproductions
With Faith on Fire
As We Come Together in Worship
Let's be Real
It Takes Time
Have You Heard?
Once Upon a Time
The Harvest Field
Yahweh Saves
Prayer as in Love
Your Word is Living
Start with God's Word
He Spoke
He's Coming for Me
True Love
Come Running
He Didn't Stop There

PREFACE

In my first collection of poems, *A Day in the Life*, I capture the joys and struggles of everyday life as a Christian working man. I have labored to be honest – sometimes raw and sarcastic, sometimes funny. This is the way life plays out. Life swings from romance to frustration, from sorrow to comedy, and back and forth between many emotions. Thus, these poems stand best as a collection rather than individually – in the context of both the joys and struggles a person faces in everyday life.

It has been a wonderful journey to write poetry about the Father and Son, about the Holy Spirit and prayer, about God's creation and the living Word, the Gospel, our faith, and what awaits us in eternity. My reflections in the second collection of poems, *Come Running*, have been driven sometimes by awe and a deep sense of worship, and sometimes by anger at the cost of sin. I do pray, however, that when Christ calls I'll come running because I have a sweet foretaste of the blessings He has in store for His people.

My Faith, My Poetry

– In Two Sets –

A Day in the Life

Come Running

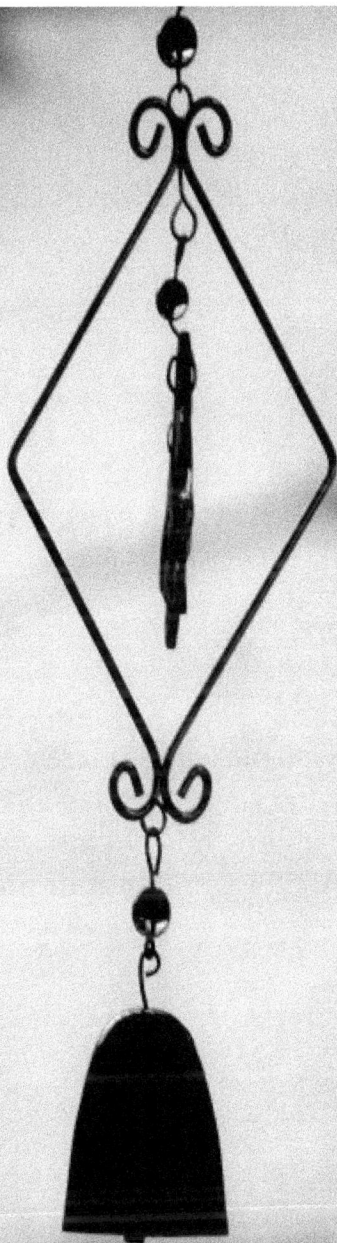

A

Day

in

the

Life

Morning at Home

In the Details

At the start of every day we need to remember that God is in the details of all that happens.

Hearts beat
Clouds form
People sleep
A kitten born

      Papers rip
      Lilies grow
      CDs skip
      Rivers flow

      If God makes His presence known
      By the ring of a telephone
      Then how much more
      In the bigger things of life

A leaf falls
A bird flies
A friend calls
A baby cries

      A pin drops
      A foot trips
      A car stops
      A clock ticks

If God cares for even me
With a cup of herbal tea
Then how much more
In the bigger things of life

God is there in the details
He is there
All I have to do is look and
He is there
If for sparrows in the trees
How much more He cares for me
God is there in the details
He is there

Into His hands I place my every care
For God is there

Starting Over
Matthew 10:39

When I get up in the morning
The first things on my mind are:
All the things I have to do,
All the places I have to be,
All the people I have to please.
They set in motion my desires for the day.
But what if I spend my time trying to start over?
Put OFF, put ON,
Put OFF, put ON;
All a part of starting over.

When I face each coming day
The first things on my mind are:
All the things I need to know,
All the books I want to read,
All the rules that apply to me.
They set in motion the commotion for the day.
What if I spend my time trying to start over?
> *Put OFF, put ON,*
> > *Put OFF, put ON;*
All a part of starting over.

Lord,
Break loose the baggage heaped upon my back.
Cut loose the chains that take up all the slack.
Make me believe *You are* the Christ
So I can start over –
And make a start at starting over with You.
I want to find my life by losing it to YOU!
> *Put OFF, put ON,*
> > *Put OFF, put ON;*
All a part of starting over with You.

Anxiety

How I despise:
The downward slope of the body since birth;
An un-welcomed tragedy that shatters security;
Selfish pride in those of whom I want to trust;
Greed and ignorance in those I'm supposed to trust;
Outright displays of evil and violence.

How I treasure:
The artistry found in the natural world;
The warm sun and a cool breeze;
A taste of clear spring water;
The aroma from a grove of pines;
Laughing with friends;
The unlimited potential we have
Dreaming and creating and discovering.

I have a constant anxiety:
What I despise could at any moment
Overwhelm all that I treasure
In life
(Until death
Gives me back all that's worth treasuring
For eternity).

Be Faithful

In all things be faithful.
In *all* things be faithful,
That Christ died and Christ arose.
Praise the Lord, oh my soul,
        And be faithful.

In all things I go through,
Oh my soul, cling to what's true
        And be faithful.

Be faithful through the highs;

Be faithful through the lows,
That Christ died and Christ arose.
Praise the Lord, He arose,
          And be faithful.

Through the ups and downs of life,
Oh my soul, cling to Christ
          And be faithful –
          As He is faithful!

The Love I've Come to Know

I thought I'd seen it all –
The sunrise in the spring, the sunset in the fall,
Moon melted shadows on the snow;
Shimmering silent shadows on the snow.
Though I enjoy the changing seasons
I miss you when you go –
For surely when you smile for me do I see
The joy that has been given to me
And the love I've come to know.

I thought I'd seen it all –
Moonrise on a golden pond, stars streaking as they
fall,
A salmon in a river's silver flow,
(A salmon in a river's silver flow).
Though I feel joy in the seasons
I miss you when you go –
For surely when you smile for me do I see

The joy that has been given to me
And the love I've come to know.

I know the world's not a perfect place,
But its problems seem to leave no trace
When that smile on your face keeps shining so;
For surely when you smile for me do I see
The joy that has been given to me
And the love I've come to know.

Off to Work

On the Bus

She became more unwelcome than her appearance
When she began reciting
The greatest piece of literature ever written –
A best seller,
A masterpiece –
At the bus stop
During rush hour.

The doors opened,
The line moved in,
And you could still hear her voice.

The crowd tensed,
Grimaced,
Threw out sarcastic comments

Because they could still hear her
Even if they couldn't see her.
Someone told her to shut up.
I guess she demanded a response,
One way or another.

Yet on the same bus
I've heard young women talk about getting loaded,
Every third word a curse,
Obnoxious and laughing coarsely.
I've smelled cigarette ashes and stale beer
Sitting next to me
And no one complained;
They just stared out the windows.
I guess this required no response –
It even preferred no response.

So I Can See

Sometimes I feel as if I'm riding on a bus–
A bus filled with people staring out the windows,
Self-absorbed in thought,
And totally unaware of each other.

Lord, give me eyes of faith
With a heart of compassion
To escape myself,
To look around
At the people riding there
Beneath Your sovereign gaze.

I know I'll never comprehend the fullness of Your
being;
Not even, all at once, what You're doing in my life.
Yet teach me what You'll have me learn today.
Show me who You'll have me love today.
Open my heart to serving You this way.
Don't let another day go by that I don't see
You're guiding me.

When Stuff Happens

Just the other day
My car broke down when I needed it most.
But, thanks to God, I was close to home.
I could have been much further down the road.

O Lord,
I set about to do things right
And stuff happens –
Snow and ice that won't go away;
Flu and cold that keep me home;
Wind and rain all night and day.
Deter,
      Distract,
            Frustrate,
                 Impact,
What I can do for You.
The way I see it and I believe it,
You don't prohibit – You set the limit
As You exhibit Your control.

But what if Satan says, "I'll show you my best.
I'll put you to the test.
Stress you out. Make you doubt.
Push you to the edge."
I need to hear You say,
"Get behind me Satan.
You're a stumbling block to me."
When stuff happens to *me!*

Say You'll set me free, Lord,
Free by Calvary.
Say You'll let me see, Lord,
See Your majesty.
When stuff happens to me, Lord,
When stuff happens to me.

Get It?

Life is..........
Achieving,
Acquiring,
More and more and more,
Again and again and again,
Because
I know I'll only lose what I gain.

Or.......
So what!
Who cares?
If I get it I get it, if I don't I don't.

I'll take it as it comes,
Watch it as it goes,
Because
I know I'll only lose it eventually.
Thus….
I become controlling, desperate, busy
Or
Complacent, apathetic, lazy.

      Will I get it?
      Perhaps not!
Jesus Christ already gave me
What I never really had,
What I'll never truly lose.

Still,
I oscillate between the two extremes
Hoping to settle somewhere in between.

Chasing

Opportunities in life are perhaps gifts that God sends our way in love. We shouldn't worry so much about keeping or losing them. We should enjoy them.

Once
He breathed
Life into Man.
Now He's blowing bubbles,
And I'm chasing them.
                    POP!

Those
I catch
I am proud of;
Those little puffs of air
On the tip of my hand.
                    POP!

I'm
Chasing,
Always chasing
Something to define me –
That is who I am.
                    POP!

I got into this game
Of chasing bubbles
He blows my way,

Like a child who
Trusts his parents
To lead him to play.

But why do I chase
In desperation?

Have I missed the point
Of why He's blowing bubbles?

He's blowing bubbles
Whether I catch them or not.
                POP, POP, POP!

In love He blows the bubbles,
And for that reason alone
I should be chasing them.

The Work Day

Everything I Touch

When *You* open my eyes
(A slave to what I see)
What I want I despise;
How shallow can I be?

When I open my mouth
I catch my words too late.

I don't like what comes out;
It's such an ugly fate.

When *You* open my ears
(To all my sinful ways)
I don't like what I hear,
Lord, even when I pray.

Are You free enough with grace
To cover my mistakes?
Are You free enough with grace
To take all that I break
And make it new?

O Lord, let me in!
When will You let me in?
Everything I touch turns to sin!

Everything there is cries for a Savior.
Everything there is, Lord, needs Your grace.
With Your law, Lord, take my nature
And beat it to the ground,
Then lift up my spirit to see Your face–
O Lord,
Lift up my spirit to see Your face!

I'm No Better

One more meeting?
Imprecision!
Lack of vision –
Indecision.

> It doesn't have to be this way,
> Yet it goes on and on and on and on,
> And on and on and on
> As I fill up with frustration.
> I want to scream.
> I want to shout!
> But I just can't get it out
> In a way that will be heard.

One more phone call?
Obfuscation.
No communication –
Procrastination.

> It doesn't have to work this way
> Yet it goes on and on and on and on,
> And on and on and on
> As I lose all confirmation.
> I want to scream.
> I want to shout!
> But I just can't get it out
> In a way that will be heard.

> *And then His Word....*

Knocks me down.
Spins me around.
Wow!
It lays me on the ground.
Who am I in *His* eyes?
I'm no better.

One more debate?
Acerbating
What's unchanging.
Still stagnating!

It doesn't have to end this way
Yet it goes on and on and on and on,
And on and on and on
As I lose my inspiration.
I want to scream.
I want to shout!
But I'll never get it out
In a way that will heard.
I'm no better.

Heart and Soul to Pursue

I don't know her very well, at all.
But something– her eyes, her voice;
I had no choice.
Maybe it was You who gave me
Her heart and soul to pursue.

The power of Your will put me in this place–
A temporary road, running on Your grace.
I must pursue
Her heart and soul for You.

Lord,
Direct our conversation – open up the door.
Reach into her heart and let her know for sure –
This love's from *You*.
Give me a Christ-like hunger, overcome my sin;
Her heart and soul to win.

I Forgot to Pray

It started out so innocently.
Then it escalated without transition.
We got to arguing on the phone again –
No turning back.

I said "Hello" conditionally.
I thought he already knew,
My own point of view –
No turning back.

But it can't stay like this – no it can't stay!
No matter who's right or wrong
I need to pray.

Though I spoke to him objectively,
He kicked into gear;

He laid out his defense, made it more intense
(A barbed wire fence),
No turning back.

I need to pray
Before that phone rings again,
Before I say anything,
Before I answer him.

It's no wonder, it's my sinful way –
I forget to pray.

Momentary Troubles

How much longer can I let my family down?
It never comes around!
How much longer can I watch others living high
When I just eke on by?
Look at what they do!
Why can't I do that, too?

There's some injustice here, such inequality
Against my family.
How much longer can I watch the good stuff pass
us by
And not give it a try?

                    Do not lose heart, my friend.
                    Fix not your eyes on what is seen
                    But on what is unseen;

Not on what is here
But on what is forever
And persevere – persevere.
For we are wasting away,
Wasting away,
And our momentary troubles
Are leading to eternal joy.

What kind of friend are you
Asking me to persevere?
Your advice is what I fear.
The way it feels to do things right
Is like spinning wheels on ice.

What kind of friend am I?
I'm leading you to Christ
And off the endless ice.

Sure Thing

As I look ahead through looking back, it's clear,
He's always near.
He paves the way from day to day –
From year to year.
And all I've ever come to be
Comes from Him, not from me!

I have a good job. I'm working eight to four.
I've put in ten years now. I'm looking for twenty
more.

But they say the world is changing –
I don't want things rearranging.

My health has been good. The worst has been the
flu.
My insurance is paid and disability, too.
Yet as I get older, every pain
Reminds me how quickly it all can change.

We have two kids - we're not planning for more.
With two cars, a dog, and a house at the shore.
I've made my plans, slow and steady.
If change comes I'll not be ready.

I don't want a risk. I want a sure thing –
To go to bed knowing what the next day brings.
Yet all I've ever come to be comes from Him,
Not from me – it comes from Him!
I've been free of risks, therefore, I worry
I'll lose the status quo.
Yet He is the One – Jesus has full control.
It passes through His hands
(In my mind) I know.

One Good Friend

You're a willing ear, always near.
We laugh and cry, never question why.
A means of grace that I embrace,
Bringing out my best, you hide the rest.

Time after time, on down the line,
People I know come and go but
One good friend.
God gave me one good friend.

I can live with *one* good friend.
Not a hero, not an angel,
Just *one* good friend.

Returning Home

Doggy Doo

The value of my home went up
The day you bought that cute little pup,
And the roses I planted
Can't compare to his aromatic gifts;
Those gifts that greet me every day
When home from work I find my way.

Doggy doo, doggy doo –
It shows how much
You love me too –
My neighbor!

Doggy doo, doggy doo –
Such love has grown
Between us two –
As neighbors!

And oh, how I feel so blessed
Every time I cut my grass.
Or the pile of sculpted scent
That bakes right into warm cement.
But best of all, my nice new shoes
Remind me how I love you too –
My neighbor!

(The day that pile grows one inch thick
I'll take up prayer and give up sleep.
I've never prayed like that before.
Who needs a church when I have next door.)

30 K High

I wrote this on an airplane (which flies about 30,000 feet high) while thinking of my wife back home.

When the movie is over, the dinner is done,
I am left all alone with that look in your eyes.
I feel just a little of what you are feeling –
It's a feeling so deep that it burns in my mind.
The thought that you're hurting is hard to imagine –
It's a thought so hard it makes me cry.
Yet sometimes I am led to believe that it's good
(It could be wishful thinking at 30 K high);
Leaving you was hard but coming home is so great
When we confirm our love and those loving sparks
fly.

It's nothing but lonely in those hotel rooms –
Propped up by pillows and resting my eyes,
Wondering where you are, what you are thinking.
Endless are these thoughts that keep stirring my
mind.
And the thought that my love could also be sleepless–
It's a thought so hard it makes me cry.
Yet sometimes I am led to believe that it's good
(Maybe wishful thinking at 30 K high);
Leaving you was hard but coming home is so great
When we confirm our love and those loving sparks
fly.

When I've packed my bags and got back on the plane,
When I'm focused on you and that look in your eyes,
I know that you're waiting to give me your love
And this is the thought that keeps strengthening my
mind.
So I hold back the thought that I bring you some
pain–
It's a thought so hard it makes me cry.
Yet sometimes I am led to believe that it's good
(Maybe wishful thinking at 30 K high);
Leaving you was hard but coming home is so great
When we confirm our love and those loving sparks
fly.

Home Base

I'm not sure we understand
What God calls me to be;
God calls me to be a godly man.
God calls me out to exercise dominion.
God sends me out – it's not my opinion.
God sends me out to all spheres of life.
God calls me out from you, my wife.

I go out to work. I go out to the world.
God calls me out– out to the world.
God sends me out
But *you* bring me back.
Day after day, night after night,
Time after time, flight after flight–
God sends me out
But *you* bring me back.

I come home to *you*. You're my home base.
I come home to *you*. With you I'm safe.
Though I go out the door, you can be sure
I come home to you.
Though I wave goodbye, every single time
I come home to you.
Don't doubt that I love you – you're my home
base.
Don't doubt that I love you – with you I'm safe.
God calls me out,
But you bring me back.
I come home to you!

I've Got You

When I stumble out of the bedroom,
Find my shoes in the hallway,
Put the trash out at the curb,
Turn on the car in the driveway;
It means the world to me to hear you say,
"I'll see you tonight."
Everyone needs someone to come home to
And I've got you.

When I leave the car at the curbside,
Shuffle home up the driveway,
There you are in the doorway
By the flowers all in bloom.
It means the world to me to hear you say,
"I'm glad you're home."
Everyone needs someone to come home to
And I've got you.

When I rise up from the table,
Sort through the latest mail,
Catch the news at eleven,
Cuddle with you on the couch;
It means the world to me to hear you say,
"I missed you today."
Everyone needs someone to come home to
And I've got you.

Everyone needs someone to come home to:
Someone to say, "I love you,"

Someone to give a hug to,
Someone to show them a little bit of heaven.
Everyone needs someone to come home to
And I've got you.

Living with a Longing for Your Love

I sat in my chair,
Listening to the sounds that echoed here and there–
Waiting, waiting for something to happen.

I wrote a letter,
Read a book and dreamt of days to come –
Waiting, waiting for something to happen.

In my heart there was a hole,
A constant stirring of my soul;
I was living with a longing for *Your* love.
Until I came to You, I never really knew
I was living with a longing for *Your* love.

I walked outside,
As night closed in, to sit beneath an apple tree –
Waiting, waiting for something to happen.

Then off to sleep
Back inside the house, another day spent –
Waiting, waiting for something to happen,
My heart was more than an open door;
I was living with a longing for *Your* love.

I couldn't see what blinded me;
I was living with a longing for *Your* love.

Dinner Together

We Need Family

How can I discuss, explain, think about, relate to "God?"
A concept, a theology, an explanation for creation.

"God," in the beginning made Man and Woman
To become one, a family.
As I grew up in family, experienced family, learned its language –
God moved from "God" to "*Abba* Father."

In father and son, bride and bridegroom, inheritance, new birth –
I am able to comprehend, communicate, consider and pursue
A relationship with Him.

The language of family leads to what we desire –
Intimacy with a personal Savior.

Though our families are not perfect we must not abandon them,
For we need the language, the experience

To speak of grace,
Of love,
And God.

Dear Jesus

Dear Jesus,
You are loved by my mommy.
You are loved by my daddy.
Someday soon I will love You just like they do.
Someday soon, Lord Jesus, someday soon.

Dear Jesus,
I know about You from my mommy.
I know about You from my daddy.
Someday soon I will know You just like they do.
Someday soon, Lord Jesus, someday soon.

Dear Jesus,
I pray at night with my mommy.
I pray at night with my daddy.
Someday soon I will pray just like they do.
Someday soon, Lord Jesus, someday soon.

Dear Jesus,
I want to serve You like my mommy.
I want to serve You like my daddy.
Someday soon I will serve You just like they do.
Someday soon, Lord Jesus, someday soon.
Someday soon, I'll stand for Jesus, just like they do.
Someday soon, Lord Jesus, someday soon.

Not to be Distinguished

Born again, two become one.
There's God's Spirit. There's human spirit
Created in His image.
We are told there are two, but in the workings
One cannot distinguish between the two
When born anew and the old self is distanced.

O Lord, it's my prayer – it's a simple prayer:
In the things that I do
I'm not to be distinguished from You.

Joined as one: there is husband, there is wife.
We can see there are two.
He blessed our earthly union and joined me to you
So that in the things we do together,
As two, we are not to be distinguished
But our old selves are distanced.

My love, it's my prayer – it's a simple prayer:
In the things that I do
I'm not to be distinguished from you.

O Spirit, it's our prayer – it's a simple prayer:
In the things that we do
We're not to be distinguished from *You.*

I Need You in My Life

Look deep into my eyes, it's not that hard to see –
It gets cloudy and confused,
Mistrusted and misused,
But all in all and in the end,
I need you in my life more than you realize.
You're my co-heir in eternity,
My complement on earth;
My listening ear – love so dear;
My sister in Christ;
My church, my body that I need,
My rib transformed for me;
Without wrinkle, without stain–
My bride in Christ.

As the Church is called to Christ,
So you are my wife –
You are essential to all that is me.

As the church is called to Christ,
You're part of my life –
You are fulfilling, you're just what I need.

Crown of Glory

O Lord, it's such an honor
(She is my crown of glory).
O Lord, here by my side
Is the source of all my pride:

Far beyond what I could do
When Your grace and love break through.

O Lord, whom have You chosen?
You chose my crown of glory to serve You–
She is my crown of glory who serves You.
Far beyond what I could do
When the power comes from You
To stir my beloved to serve You.

O Lord, gold has no reign
When she glorifies Your name.
Far beyond what I could do
When the power comes from You,
She is my crown of glory
Who serves You.

Evening Chaos

Marriage is Hard Work

He took us to his chambers.
He gave us his advice.
He said, "Marriage is hard work.
I'll only say it twice –
Marriage is hard work!
Now treat each other nice."

We can't be together for too long;
What needs to be said comes out all wrong
Or never sees the light of day,
And the things I shouldn't say are said anyway.

An endless cycle, just us two,
Though I try to open up to you.
I'll share my deepest thoughts some day
When the things I shouldn't say have all gone away.

Work, work, work – marriage is hard work.
I work at her. She works at me.
We never really see that work is not the mission,
The answer is submission to the Lord.

Wrestling for Control

He speeds up.
  She slows down.
He gets lost.
  She gets found.
He says, "Save."
  She says, "Buy."
He'll give in.
  She'll still try
  For control.

She says, "Yes."
  He says, "No."
She says, "Stop."

He says, "Go."
Her few words
    To *his* book.
She looks down
    From *his* look
    Of control.

Around and around and around and around
And around we go.

God says, "Give."
    I receive.
God says, "Faith."
    "I" believe.
God says, "Fast."
    "Not *my* plate!"
God says, "Ask."
    I can't wait
        For control.

I say, "Run."
    God says, "Walk."
I can't hear
    When *God* talks.

It's so subtle but it colors all that we do.
It's a knee-jerk, Jonah-like response
That comes from a rebellious heart
Always wrestling with God for control.
And we wrestle with each other
As we wrestle with God for control.

Things on My List

Husband to Wife:
>Hey honey,
>I'm up and out of bed – ready to go.
>What do you need from me?
>Is it okay if I do some of the things on my list
>While I'm waiting?
>Be assured my dear,
>You are the first in line.
>You'll have all of my time –
>*All* of my time.

Husband in Prayer:
>Hey Lord,
>I have a list of things for us to do,
>And I made up the list with You in mind.
>If *my* list is really good could You make it her
>list, too?
>Isn't this how it goes?
>Any other way I just don't know.

Wife to Husband:
>Hey lovies,
>I'd like to plan ahead two weeks from now.
>The calendar's still free. Is it okay?
>I will need to call around, at this time, to set
>the date.

Wife in Prayer:
>Hey Lord,

Should I wait for *You* to act on him?
He doesn't move too fast;
Doesn't plan ahead– just decides what he
will do
In his time, rather than mine.

And the things on my list
Are not the things on his list.
I'm sure the things on *Your* list
Are different still.

Think Like I Think

It was a revelation to me when I realized that others do not think like I think. It might sound funny, but it's true. The book of James has much to say about this.

I used to analyze everything you said
As if your words, from my mind, were read.
You talk and talk and talk off the top of your head.
I think and think and think, think and think and think,
Think and think and think – don't say anything instead.

My mind works clockwise; yours, counter clockwise.
You think out loud while I analyze.

51

In the north the water swirls opposite from the
south.
Love can seem so different when it issues from the
mouth.
Knowing what James said on how it's going to be,
I must be quick to forgive when you talk to me.

If we bridle the mouth, we bridle the body–
Control the ship's rudder and it stays on course.
A very small spark can set a great fire.
We can tame the earth– tame *all* of the earth–
But we can't tame the tongue.

What a liberating thought to know you don't think
like I think.
      Think like I think?
          Think like I think?
              I thank God I found out
                  You don't think like I
                    think.

You are the One

I know it's late, there's sleep in your eyes –
But you are the one to hear my heart's cry.
You are not afraid to give up yourself –
To be the one to take love off the shelf.
You build the bridge on back to my youth –
By listening well you walk in my shoes.
You are the one who listens to me.

You are the one who hears my heart's beat.
You take the time to hear what I say.
                You are the one – God sent you my
                way.

Love comes by listening.
Healing comes from hearing.
Without saying a word, *you are* the one.

Trust Me

There's a great divide between us –
It came from somewhere I don't know.
But I'm here reaching out my hand,
Saying, "Trust me."

You're speechless for now,
Yet there's something still inside
And I'm here waiting patiently,
Saying, "Trust me."

Haven't I shown you that I care?
Haven't I told you that I'm here?
Haven't I loved you all these years –
                        All these years?
It should be easy, so I thought,
When there's someone to hold on to –
So I'm here right beside you
Saying, "Trust me."

Yet in a small way, just a little bit, I know how Jesus feels
As He calls out to *me* everyday,
Saying, "Trust me."

If Ever There Was a Night

Do you keep trying to show God that you can do better, that you can do it all by yourself? Remember what happened to Peter (Luke 22:31-34).

Tonight, unlike any other night,
Wait and see –
I'm staying in the light, tonight.
Tonight, I'm staying a saint.
The sinner I ain't, tonight.

You're always watching me, guiding me.
Take a break for Your sake.
Give me space, tonight.

Tonight, I'll go it alone,
I know I can –
I feel it in my bones, tonight.
Tonight, no sin or snare
Is gonna catch me unaware, tonight.

Why don't You call in sick, stay in bed,
Take time off from my head?
I'll be okay, tonight.

Tonight, if ever there was a night
I'm in the zone.
Tonight, If ever there was a night
I can go it alone.

> Every where I turn, every time I dream,
>   every step I take;
> If I could do it all over again, take one more
>   turn to be
> I wouldn't do what I did the way I did
> So give me a chance..... tonight!
>   I can go it alone, tonight.

Bedtime

At the End of the Day

O Lord, what have You given me here
To mark the days that pass?
When I sit beside this child of Yours
All the problems of life roll past.
A moment so filled with warmth and joy–
In the soft light, quiet of the night;
So peaceful, so still,
With her hair draped softly upon the pillow;
Eyes so tenderly closed.
At the end of the day You meet my needs.
At the end of the day
When my child before me sleeps.
Knowing I'm here, she sleeps.

When in my heart I realize how much I love her
I stand in awe of how much, O Lord,
You must love me.

O Lord, what have You created in me
To mark the days that pass?
Will You stay beside this child of Yours
So the problems I make don't last?
A moment so filled with warmth and joy–
In the soft light, quiet of the night;
So peaceful, so still,
My head so softly upon my pillow;
My eyes so heavily closed.
At the end of the day You meet my needs.
At the end of the day when Your child before You
sleeps.
Knowing You're here, I sleep.

When in my heart I realize how much I love You,
I stand in awe of how much, O Lord,
You must love me.

Look Beyond Me

There was a time I'd hold your hand,
Without a word, so gently tight.
Just being there beside your bed
Would calm you down and make things right.

There was a time I'd stay awake

So you would know you're not alone.
I would leave the night-light on
So you could fall asleep, at home.

There was a time I'd hold you still
Here in my arms close to my heart.
Yet there is One beyond our days
Who holds you now when we're apart.

Just as the stars up in the sky
Go way beyond what we can see,
The greatest peace that I can give
Is in the love that's beyond me.

That's What Daddies Do

I see sunshine, you see rain.
I see parting clouds, you feel pain –
For now, but that will change,
That will change.

I choose colors over shades of gray.
You wear black to school every day –
For now, but that will change,
That will change.

And while you're waiting for life to change,
I'll wait with you –
That's what daddies do.

I see friendships that grow and stay.
You see no one with you today –
For now, but that will change,
That will change.

I know love will come your way.
Your heart's sad and lonely today –
For now, but that will change,
That will change.

And while you're waiting for life to change,
I'll wait with you –
That's what daddies do.

From now until there's no more change,
There's one thing that will stay the same –
"I love you."
He loves you, too.
That's what daddies do.

I see a storm that will blow away.
Your worst fear, it's here to stay –
For now, but that will change,
That will change.

And while you're waiting for life to change,
I'll wait with you –
That's what daddies do.

God's Gift to a Lonely World

Unarmed, unafraid –
That's how I feel, unashamed.
She has the gift to draw me in
  And win me over.

Like an angel on the wind,
A heart in heaven yet she fits right in.
With just her eyes she lifts me up
  And wins me over.

Innocent, unaware –
That's how she is and I don't care.
She has the gift to draw me in
  And win me over.

Like Solomon's Pomade

They bathed her six months in oil of myrrh.
In perfume she was six months more–
In preparation for the king; a presentation to the king.

Once we were lovers in the night;
Our fragrance was fleeting and light.
But now you are everlasting.
Your scent is so sweet and lasting.
(I feel like a king when I'm in your presence:
Call me Solomon, smell your fragrance.)

You are the fragrance of many years–
A pomade of sad and happy tears.
A fragrant bride you are to me–
Still a bride you are to me.

I'll be Solomon, you can be my bride,
And our song of songs will fill the air.
Nothing will compare– *nothing will compare!*
For how much better than wine is your love,
And the scent of you than all perfume.

Eternal Love Divine

Song of Solomon

Bridegroom:
> How beautiful you are, my darling,
> For your eyes are like the doves.
> You're a lily in thorns, my darling,
> And your voice is sweet to me.
> How beautiful you are, my darling,
> I can find no flaw in you.
> You're more pleasing than wine, my darling–
> More fragrant than any spice.

Bride:
> Oh how handsome you are, my lover.
> Your name is perfume poured forth.
> And I belong to you, my husband –
> Your desire is for me.

Oh how handsome you are, my lover,
And I delight in your shade.
You're like an apple tree, my husband,
In a forest of young men.

Wedding Guests:

We rejoice and delight in You.
We praise Your love more than wine –
That love here on earth would foreshadow
His eternal love, divine.

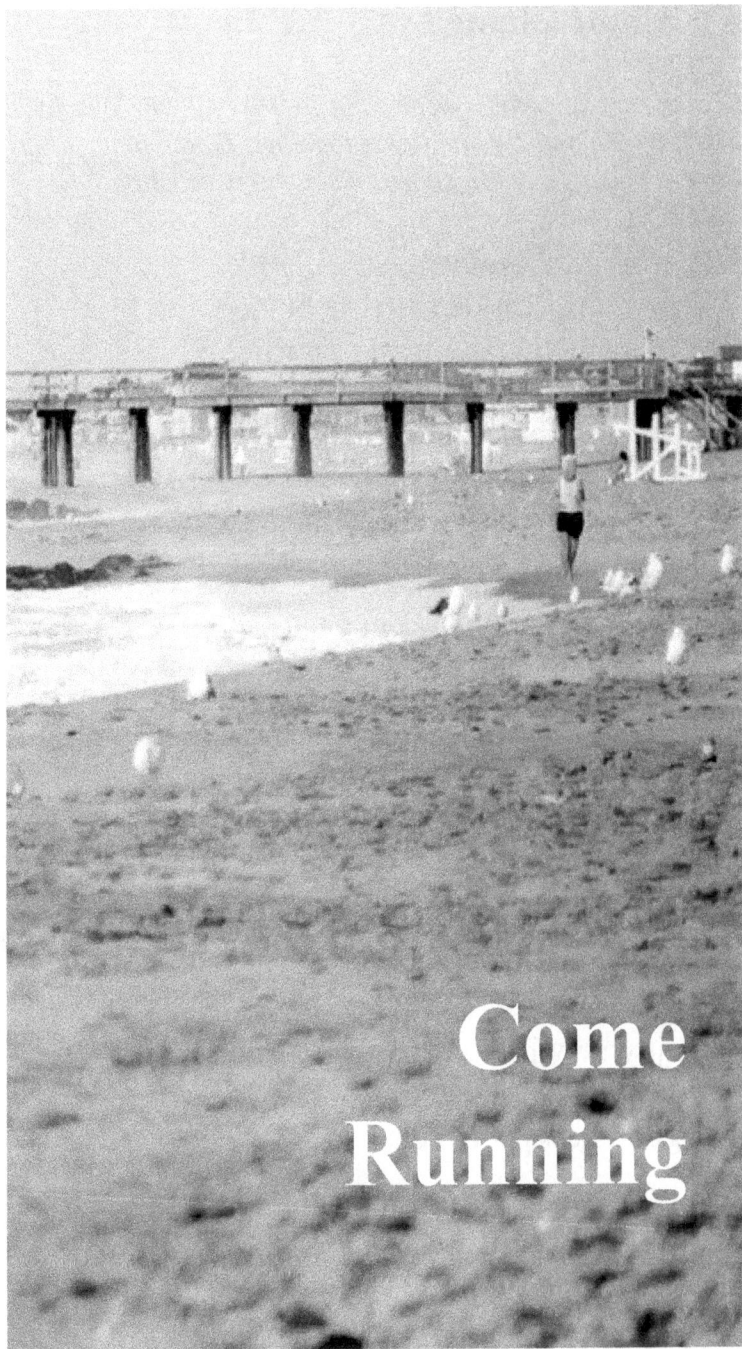

Come
Running

All About Change

God moves all things according to His will for our lives individually and for our lives together. God's plan for us involves change, a directional change toward Him.

Therefore, my brothers,
When you reflect on Christ
You make yourself a living sacrifice
To renew your mind
And be transformed to worship the Lord.

———————∞———————

I had no choice.
What's done is done – I'm a chosen one.
But, it doesn't stop there!
I was reborn for change, made free to change.
He won't let go. He told me so.
It's all about change.
And the good news is I'll change.

Repentance, forgiveness, continuous change;
A newness, freeness, directional change;
To become like Christ is all about change.
To enjoy new life is all about change.
Let go and grow, one thing I know –
The good news is I'll change.

The Potter, the clay, raised from the grave;
Rebirth, new earth, destined for change;
The catalyst, the cross, there's gain and there's loss –

The good news is I'll change.
It's coming, get ready – it's change.
From day to day, don't turn it away –
It's change.
It's all about change,
And the good news is we'll change.

In His Image

When I look down at solid ground,
I'm not surprised – it's always there.
I can't imagine where I would be without it there.
In our lives there's always time
As we come and go – though nothing's done.
We still connect Father to father, and Son to son.

It's by design: something we share
In the way we live or the words we speak;
More than we know from day to day, and week to
week.
Some people say, mixed in with me
Is a bit of you – that's no surprise.
There's a bit of Him I can see in your loving eyes.

I stopped by and let myself in.
The house was empty, I sat in your chair,
Watched the news, picked up the paper – without
you there.
Father to father, Son to son –
It all comes together in *His* image.

Earth and Body

This poem gives glory to God for his wonderful creation such as seen on the earth or observed in the human body.

wavy wind blown clouds
bring forth color
to the face of the sky
warmed by the sun
suspended for all to behold
by smooth masts of wood
over undulating hills and valleys
and striations of formations
a deep ocean draws my eyes
and brings forth
the flowing movement of rivers
down to the white beaches
across the curvature of the land

she moves
forward
with
wispy hair
soft silken lips
set in a blushing face
cradled atop a pedestal to behold
beneath which balances
rhythmic breasts
undulating ribs
a naval

to draw my eyes
accentuating the curvature
of her hips and derriere
flowing to the thighs
all held aloft
by strong
calves
upon smooth
tender
soles

the transcendent and awesome Creator deserves
my greatest praise!

Get On With It

Sometimes we know Him by what He is not:
His goodness in evil seeing;
His great love by sorrow feeling;
His mercy in judgment being.

God does not promise that life will get better,
But we can get better at growing in knowing Him
And enjoying Him now.

Consider.......
What is behind a husband and wife?
What's at the core? What are laws for?
Look all around at nature's design!
Who can say he's captured the mind?

What's life and death? What makes good and bad?
Who can predict who's happy and sad?

Everything in life boils down to this,
There are two things that lead to bliss:
Knowing Him better and enjoying Him forever.
     Simply,
           Get on with it!
All that there is (a yellow brick road),
Leads to growing in knowing Him
And enjoying Him now.

All that we are (heart, mind and soul),
Must be growing in knowing Him
And enjoying Him now.

Extinction

Ph.D.s and 'ologists scraping and dusting
The sedimentary rock;
Burnt and hot, and desperate for a single clue.
Such a leap of faith to a missing link
When all around,
Even the crumbling rock cries out –
The very creation cries out, "We have a Creator!"
The Devil put Darwin on a death track –
A theory without fact.
A faith in no god, no hope,
No good to anyone.

Principals and teachers, writing and erasing
On dusty black boards;
Proud and bold and desperate for a single clue.
Such a leap of faith to a missing link
When all around,
Even the smallest child cries out–
The very creation cries out, "We have a Creator!"

Faith or fiction?
They'd better make a clear distinction
Or face their own extinction.

Fix Your Thoughts on Me

BEFORE you shun temptation's dare,
Fix your thoughts – for I am there.

BEFORE you feed and clothe the poor,
Fix your thoughts – on heaven's store.

BEFORE you pray for healing, peace,
Fix your thoughts – I love my sheep.

BEFORE you go and fight for Me,
Fix your thoughts – on Calvary.

BEFORE you cry, "Let justice reign!"
Fix your thoughts – I rose again.

Let your thoughts be fixed on Me.

Let your heart my mercy see.
I came that you may know the way.
Fix your thoughts on Me, today.

Cup Bearer
John 18:7-11

There once was a king who was too afraid to drink,
In fear for his life I think.
He chose himself a man to stand in his place:
"Take this cup from me.
Nehemiah, take this cup from me!"

There once was a King who took away *my* drink,
In fear for my life I think.
Cup of wrath in hand, He stood in my place:
"Take this cup from me.
My Father, take this cup from me."

Now the cup that is mine is sweet, sweet as wine –
Full of life, sweet sacrifice.
He is *my* Christ – who gave His life for me.

Until You Came to Me

At Your tomb, Mary heard You call her name.
Out at sea, Peter heard You call his name.
As for me, until I heard You call my name
I couldn't come to You.

Who am I but a sinner in Your eyes.
What have I but idols You despise.
How could I even think that I could try
To come to You?

Now every day in wondrous ways
I look to You, for it is true
That until You came to me I couldn't come to You.

Wake Up, Rise Up
Ephesians 5:8-21

Wake up, rise up if you are sleeping –
Let the love of Christ shine through.
Nothing escapes the eyes of the Lord.

Wake up, rise up, let the darkness flee.
Be true to one another
And look into the eyes of the Lord.

Wake up, rise up always with thanksgiving
And psalms, hymns, and praise.
Nothing escapes the ears of the Lord.

Wake up, rise up above your foolish ways.
Turn now from your sin
And look into the eyes of the Lord.

O sleeper, sleep no more.
Rise up from your bed,

Cast off your sin instead
And let the Lord of truth be your morning sun –
Wake up, rise up – *sleep no more!*

Cause Me to Grow

Children get into trouble easily because they haven't yet learned how to put a mask over their sinful desires. Adults learn how to camouflage sin and that makes it harder to dig out the sin and deal with it.

How long have I been asleep in the pew?
I've taught and sought and served,
I've fed the few.
But when I pray I hear the words of a child,
A proud and selfish child.
I've come full circle, I fear I've not grown wiser.

How long have I been repentant askew?
I've prayed, been saved, believed –
"I'm born anew!"
The hardest sins were first to go. Now I know,
Getting older means
Getting better at masking what really matters.

Although I can justify everything I do,
I was fooled.
It's not how it is supposed to be –
I thought the hardest sins went first
And life got easier.

Lord, bare my soul,
Dig way down deep,
Go way down low.
Pull out those sins I won't let go.
Dig deeper and deeper,
Deeper and deeper;
Cause me to grow,
Lord, cause me to grow.

Maturity

The basic message is simple,
Wouldn't you agree?
How else could we hear it!
The Spirit didn't call us as intellects,
He opened our hearts *to love*.

When it comes to maturity
I believe that our Father satisfies us one by one
According to His design.
Whether a driven mind or a curious child,
One by one we enjoy Him.

Maybe it's as simple as it can be.
Maturity is relational –
A father and his child,
A bride and her groom,
Two friends, two brothers,
Our Christ.
I trust Him.

I love Him.
I put all my faith in Him.
Everything else can be a distraction.

Maturity, we should rate
On *how* we relate.

Mystery of Mysteries

In the beginning there was the Word,
And He was with God,
And He was God.
Through Him all things were made.
In Him was all of life.
From Him came all of light
Since the beginning days.

Trinity, exists eternally:
God in three defines reality.
Trinity, has personality:
One and three, relationally.

Mystery of mysteries: the Holy Trinity –
Exists supernaturally, yet comes alive to me.
   I can't define it.
     I can't explain it.
       I can't defend it.
         I just believe it.
Mystery of mysteries: the Holy Trinity –
Exists supernaturally, by grace that I can see.

'Isms

How far some people go to make a world apart
From the one true God through *'isms*.
Taoism, Marxism, Socialism, Humanism, Atheism,
Agnosticism –
Life is a prism
Of world views defined by the human mind
In *'isms*.

Even within religion there's division:
Judaism, Calvinism, Arminianism,
Pelagianism, Catholicism, Protestantism.
Can I believe what I want to believe?
How naïve!

Narrow is the road that leads to life through Jesus
Christ.

And if I say I have no faith, I fool myself –
There's something I believe in.
Face it, place it where it belongs.
Chase it, trace it right or wrong.
No one lives *'ism*-less.

Who Pursues Whom?
Psalms 42 and 43

Who pursues whom?
I'm an outcast in a strange land.

Who pursues whom?
I'm forgotten amid the waves.
Who pursues whom?
It's my bones that are breaking
And I hate this place.

Who pursues whom
When my soul is so downcast?
Who pursues whom
When my soul is stirred within me?
Yet I praise You,
My Messiah who pursues.

I've been cast out from the Temple, beyond the
mount of snow
To a land where I am taunted, "Your God will never
show."
My Messiah, come pursue me. I wait, but I cannot
hide:
Beyond the gates of heaven, beyond the Father's side.

Oh to be in Your presence is where I long to be.
Oh to be in Your presence, there's no better place
for me.
I've a passion for Your presence; I've tasted it
before.
Like the aftertaste of wine I need more!

Better to Receive

Is it ever out of love we give,
If love we can't accept –
Freely accept?

Think about it –
Is it really better to give,
When the greatest love of all
We receive?

There is nothing we can give
In return for His love.
Nothing to give,
Only to receive in faith,
By grace undeserved.

Love is a gift that grows out of the love
We receive.

Why Did You Go?

Bars and scars.
Imprisoned. In fear.
So close to death,
No friends near.
Three times beaten
By rods. Stoned.
Cold and naked
Without a home.

Night and day
On the open sea.
Shipwrecked. Left
Without a plea.
Danger came
From fellow men.
Ragged, crippled,
To Jerusalem.

Forty lashes
But minus one.
What was worse?
True brothers none.

Hunger, thirst
And suffering so.
Lack of sleep
For a church to grow.

Tell me, Paul,
Why did you go?
Is this love
Something I can know?
Realizing all
That you would face,
Why did you go
In your Master's place?

It's not natural!
It's not normal!

Shattered. Battered.
It must have mattered.

Tell me, Paul,
Why did you go?
I would have given up
Long ago.

Tell me, Paul,
Why did you go?
Such deep, deep love
I need to know.

Clay Reproductions

And so the Father agreed
With His Son and Spirit,
To begin
Complementary reproductions
Of His image
Using earth (dirt, clay)
And placing inside of each
A priceless treasure –
The aroma of life.
Each artistic reproduction is unique
And wonderful.
But why not use marble or granite?
Why use a sedimentary deposit?
Drop it and it breaks.
It cracks and gets holes in it

So that the priceless treasure leaks out.
Were we not to preserve
The aroma of life
Until He returns –
So that we could anoint Him?

With Faith on Fire
John 8: 42-47

Satan the snake, He lied to Eve;
Got her to eat from the tree.
We were drawn in through Adam's sin
Into a lie.
It was a lie that ruined him.

The master of lies is in the world;
Powerful men to him will turn.
In Christ we've found our solid ground.
We're not enslaved,
We have been saved: to truth we're bound.

Satan will lie to you and me –
Get us to sin in secrecy.
Together let's stand with upraised hands.
In fellowship true, God's light shines through
To bless our land.

When we're filled with the truth
There's no room for the lies.
There's no room, can't be fooled, with faith on fire.

When we're on fire for the Lord,
When we are right on the Word,
The lies can't win – can't enter in with faith on fire.

We are brothers in the Lord.
We are sisters of the Word.
By the Spirit we can hear –
O Lord of truth, draw us near!
Take my hand, let us stand with faith on fire.

As We Come Together in Worship

As we come together in worship,
As we gather to pray and sing,
May our pride be gently broken
As we turn to Christ our King.

As we gather in thanksgiving
May we gather in His love.
As we come together in worship
May He bless us from above.

Let our praises rise to Heaven,
More lasting than the dew;
And with repentant hearts
Let our faith be found anew.

As we come together in worship,
What wonders we will gain –
For precious is the hope

That He will come again.
Countless are His blessings,
Priceless is His love,
Amazing is His grace –
All treasures from above.

Let's Be Real
Proverbs 27:17

Listen to *all* that I say –
Not every word will be in place.
It is my heart that you must face.
Then just between us two –
You and me in privacy
With nothing but sincerity,
No one else we need to be –
Let's be real!

Let's serve God – let's be real.
There's no proof text to what I feel.
There's no one else we need to see
But J.C.
Let's be real: pray with zeal;
Live and heal; love and feel
All that's real.
Let's be real!

It Takes Time

Off with the jeans and on with the slacks,
I'll trade in my chains for a tie off the rack.
You can dress me up and take me to church
But I'll make the same mistakes.
I'll carry my foolish pride
And wear it well on the outside.

So what if I come to church on Sunday
In oversized pants and tri-colored braids?
What if I dress down and meet you at church?
What will they say – I'm like my clothes?
I still carry plenty of sin
And wear it well outside in.

Does it matter if you only see what I want you to
see,
Without seeing me?

It takes time to change inside out,
To put off the old and put on the new.
How naïve, we believe it's easy to do.

Yet Jesus said,
"I am with you always,
Even to the end of time."

Have You Heard?

Always was, always is, always will be;
Changing lives, changing worlds, changing
history.
It moves and it spreads through space and time,
And it tastes to the poor like the best of wine.

Have you heard the WORD?
Has it changed your life?
Have you heard?

Ear to ear, heart to heart, tongue to tongue;
Carries hope, carries peace, carries the Son.
It's our light in the darkness,
A guide through all our days.
It's the answer to our questions, it's the Way.

It's the good news.
It's the true news.
Have you heard?

It's the *WORD!*

Once Upon a Time

Once upon a time,
Thousands of years ago,
We only knew the Lord our God
By the nameless name "I am,"

For He was beyond our ability to understand.

Once upon a time,
Not quite so long ago,
We came to know the Lord our God
At the sacred cross of Christ
Where He gave us our ability to understand.

Yet today I get lost in the troubles of my life,
Where I lose sight of the great "I am"
And I lose sight of who I am.

I am
Not defined by my past.
I am
Not defined by my scars.
I am a child of the living God!
I know Him as *my* Savior.
I know Him as *my* Lord.
He is my great Redeemer,
My source of love, my living Word.

The Harvest Field

Imagine waking up one morning, stepping onto the porch of your house and being surprised by a vast, full grown field of wheat spreading out from horizon to horizon. You had no part in its growing nor in its planting. It's there, just waiting to be harvested.

God opened my eyes to see the sun rise
Upon the harvest field:
Stretching out as far as I could see
Endless is the harvest field.

Why do I live like I don't know
The field's abundant and fully grown?
In God's love the seeds were sown –
Now there's a harvest!

Come out with me to the harvest.
The field's all grown – it's a harvest.
All that's needed is to harvest;
Let's go out and bring the harvest home.

Let's go and pray amid the harvest –
Touch and sway with the harvest.
God's love is vast as the harvest;
Come and bring the harvest home.
Let's go out and bring
The harvest home.

Yahweh Saves

When I'm too weak to bend my knees,
When I can't pray He comes to me.
My precious Lord who loves me so,
He warms my heart when it grows cold.

The *name* of Jesus is my prayer.
His name alone is my prayer.

When I can't pray, *Yahweh saves*.

Prayer as in Love

Do we pursue love
     The way we pursue prayer?

          Predictable
          Controlled
          No disturbances
          A quiet time
          Everyone knows and agrees
          This time is for prayer
          Set aside and special
          Separate from life

Or should we desire prayer
     The way we desire love?

A kiss
An embrace
Sometimes short and sweet
Sometimes intense
A touch
Every opportunity
Even in our dreams
Woven into life itself
Inseparable

Your Word is Living

No matter how eloquent and creative I am with language, I fail miserably in capturing the majesty and power of God's Word. In this work, I contrast how human words can paint beautiful pictures yet still be so powerless to bring new life to broken hearts. Words might trigger the mind and its senses but they fall lifeless in the heart unless the Spirit of God bears them there.

It's the traveling sun that paints a line
Between the nights and days,
Colors the clouds that hang dimension
While slowly on their way –
That reflects a dreamer's path
Where runs the every eye
On across the painted waters
To where they meet the sky.

I watched a butterfly cross a field
In dancing, fluttering flight –
To espy a little flower on which
So gently to alight.
I drifted on a mountain's lake
By mercy of the wind,
Rippling the reflections in hopes
The lake would part a glimpse.
I watched a storm pass.
I looked for reasons.
I searched reflections –
Not looking, dreaming.

I stumbled through rows of bladed grass –
Hollow logs, and dandelions.
I crumpled through many empty days
And through the leaves of time.
But in the morning's freshness
As in the past night's dreams,
Strung the words throughout my mind –
Words that I must weave:
Silken words of love that touch
Like kisses when they're said;
On glistening tears of love
Braided gently along the web.

No matter how hard I tried
My words escaped my dreams and died.

Your Word is living! My words are dead.
Your Word breathes life simply when it's said.

My words are like dreams in my head.
What can I say? What can I say?
My words just stumble and crumble
And die away.

Start with God's Word

When questions arise,
When tears fill your eyes,
When no one seems to have the answer;
When you can't make sense
From what has no sense,
Who can you go to but our Master.

There's one place to start;
It's not with the heart,
And it's not with your own clear reason.
Where do you begin
To search out your sin?
If not with the King then it's treason!

Don't come asking me.
Don't claim that you're free.
You're bound to the order He created.
Your freedom lies there
When you're in His care –
When it is He to whom you're related.

When based on your view
You choose what to do,

Don't blame Him if you're on the wrong bus.
There's only one truth –
Doesn't take a sleuth:
It's revealed; it's changeless through Jesus.

You've got to start with God's Word –
It's the only way to explain this world.
It's the *only way* to explain this world.

He Spoke

In the beginning
God created the heavens and the earth,
And oh, *it was good!*

Spirit, apostle, prophet, Lord,
Burning bush, written Word –
Doesn't it ever make you wonder?
Don't you really want to know?
How is it that He spoke and it came to be?

He spoke and life came forth.
He spoke in day and night.
He spoke to fill the earth.
He spoke to give us light.

He spoke law into stone.
He spoke the blind to see.
He spoke, a kingdom come.
He spoke – it came to be.

He spoke and blessed the womb.
He spoke a rainbow sign.
He spoke Christ from the tomb.
He spoke to govern time.

He spoke, the heavens made.
He spoke and calmed the sea.
He spoke, the price was paid.
He spoke and set us free.

From the first word ever spoken
To the last word yet to come,
His Word is alive and causing
His will to be done.

He's Coming for Me

My risen Lord is both
Too glorious to behold
And the Lamb that was slain,
Unrecognizable
Yet bearing the marks of the cross.
As if He remembers;
As if He's waiting for me.

Is not my Lord defined
Forever by His past
While Creator of it all?
A timely resurrection yet,
So timeless, so priceless.

As if He remembers;
As if He's waiting for me.

I'm bearing scars, known for sin,
Carrying a past, I'm fallen again.
It matters not, He's coming for me.
Just as I am, He's coming for me.

The atonement is true, He's coming for me.
God's wrath subdued, He's coming for me.
Still bearing the marks, He's coming for me.
Again in body form, He's coming for me.
To fulfill and redeem, He's coming for me.
Forgiven, complete – He's coming for me.
Past and all, marked by the Fall,
Just as I am, He's coming for me.

True Love

I've always had this hole in my heart
I've tried every way to fill;
With trophies,
Possessions,
And friends
By my will.
While all the time
True love
Had already come:
In a baby,
A priest,

A dying man,
A risen king.

True love took up His cross
And died for me.
True love gave up His life
To set me free.
True love can't be returned,
Won or bought,
Or even learned.
True love
Is a gift from God
To be received.

Come Running

The wedding day has come.
The bride runs down the aisle to her groom –
(A marriage made in heaven)
And she runs, she runs.
Oh I'm waiting for my day to come when He calls
to me
And I come running.

Picture this:
Water flowing cool and clear,
Safe inside a perfect sphere.
Home at last in a city made in heaven
Where angels guard the way
To streets of gold as pure as glass.

And if you can picture this,
Come running!

Picture this:
Precious stones in all of sight.
No sun or moon, God is the Light.
Behold the Lamb in a garden made in heaven
Where the fruit is sweet,
Where the curse is lifted from the land.
Picture this and if you can,
Come running!

Picture this:
Open gates, never closed –
Nothing impure, even gold.
Walking 'neath the tree of life.
Sitting at the feet of Christ.
Love reclaimed, called forth by name –
Come running!

Picture this:
God's presence restored,
Restored at last.
And if you can picture that,
Come running!

He Didn't Stop There

God created us in His image
And gave us dominion over the rest of His creation,
    But He didn't stop there.

God forgave us our sins
And covered us with the blood of Christ,
    But He didn't stop there.

God gave us guidelines by which to live and love
And the power to make it real,
    But He didn't stop there.

God secured for us a place in eternity
And promised that it would be heavenly.
And when we finally get to Heaven,
We'll find.......
    He didn't stop there.

Healthy Life Press

Books, eBooks, DVDs

Golden, Colorado

A Small, Independent Christian Publisher with a big mission—to help people live healthier lives physically, emotionally, spiritually, and relationally.

For a downloadable PDF catalog of our resources, and access to free sample excerpts from our books, visit: *www.healthylifepress.com*

1-877 331-2766 | *info@healthylifepress.com*

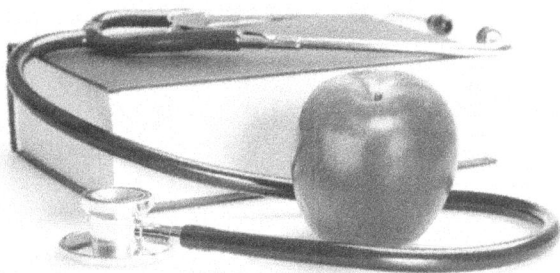